DIY gifts in jars

30 Simple, Delicious, Inexpensive Gifts in Jars Recipes

DISCLAIMER

Introduction

DIY Gifts in Jars allows you to completely personalize your next round of gift-giving with thirty delightful recipes dolled up and decorated in beautiful, artistic Mason jars. Bring the warmth and joy of cookie-baking and snacking to your friends who don't have the time to put the recipes together themselves; lend your grandmother her essential mulled wine recipe, complete with tons of spices, cloves, and step-by-step instructions to create the final mulled wine delight. Bring cakes, brownies, blondies, snacks, and breads into the homes and hearts of your friends and family on their birthdays, their special holidays, their break up days, and their happy days. No matter the occasion, these DIY gifts put smiles on faces and happiness in bellies, guaranteed.

Understand, however, that creating priceless gifts in jars can be a bit challenging. Tossing a bunch of flour in a jar and throwing it toward your family members doesn't exactly cut it. Luckily, this book provides answers to all of your decorating and recipe-formulating questions. It allows you to understand:

1. Where to find your jars.
2. How to clean your jars.
3. The best ways to decorate your jars.
4. How many weeks you can store the jars before gifting them.
5. How to assemble the recipes as you go along.
6. How to decorate your jars.

Bring beautiful patterns of chocolate chips, cranberries, cherries, cocoa, nutmeg, and all the most wonderful-smelling items into a Mason jar. Wrap the Mason jar with stunning decorations and personalize your gift to your family and friends. Your gifts will rise to the occasion of all holidays and will bring happiness and inspiration into every event.

Time of Contents

CHAPTER #1
DIY gifts in jars
preparation

Take a step into the creative gift zone with DIY gifts in jars. There's no better way to personalize your gifts to your best friends and family members than with groovy, decorated jars filled with sweet stuff. These gifts are essential for all-year-round giving: from birthdays to Valentine's Day; from Halloween to the end of the year holidays.

Of course, making gifts in jars and making them look "desirable" for your friend or family member is a little bit tricky. Refine your gift-creating tasks, and understand how to better improve your creative gifts-in-jars maneuvers with the following helpful hints and tricks.

Frequently Asked Questions:

1. Where should I look for canning jars?
Look in the baking aisle at your local supermarket, your local hardware store, and various home goods stores. Remember to choose jars that are wide-mouthed for better ease while filling the jars.

2. How do I pack full recipes in these jars?
As you know, each jar can only hold about four cups worth of anything. Look to recipes that call

for only approximately 2 ½ cups of flour along with only one or two cups of sugar. You can usually sift the flour to allow it to pack better in the bottom of the jar. Also, you can alter the overall recipe to align better with your specific-sized jar. For example, if you need to completely halve the recipe, you must make the recipe that you attach to the jar fit with this change. If the original recipe calls for 4 cups of flour and four eggs, you must pour only two cups of flour into the jar and write "2 eggs" on the provided recipe.

3. How far ahead of time should I make these gifts in jars?

Remember that most mixes with sugars or brown sugars will start to harden up after about three weeks. Furthermore, chocolate tends to look a little bulbous after about a month. Therefore, try to make your jar gift recipes only a few days before you plan to gift them.

How to Clean Your Gift Jars

Before you utilize your mason jars for gift-giving, you should completely sterilize them. This promotes healthy future baking.

1. Begin by washing the jars, the bands, and the lids with soapy water. Completely rinse them.

2. Next, position each jar in a big pot with their heads up. Cover the jars with water and place the pot on the stovetop.

2. Place the stovetop on HIGH and allow the water to boil for fifteen minutes.

4. Next, turn off the heat and toss the lids in the pot, as well. Leave everything in the water for ten minutes.

5. Lastly, remove the jars from the water with tongs, and allow them to cool and dry on clean paper towels.

Ideas to Decorate Your Gift Jars

Gifts in Jars decorations make or break the overall gift. It doesn't matter how delicious that brownie mix is; if the exterior jar doesn't include a fancy ribbon (or some such design), your gift is going to look a little lackluster. Look to the following gifts in jars decorating tips for assistance!

1. Twine: The Decorating Essential

Twine is super-cheap and brings that farmer-down-home element to your gift-giving approach. Wrap the twine around the top of the jar and tie it in a pretty bow, and attach the recipe to the bow; alternately, plaster a square piece of pretty cloth to the top of your jar and secure the cloth with the twine. Remember to always utilize a bigger square piece of cloth than what would regularly cover your jar. You want it to bundle up around the top to create texture.

2. Chalkboard Your Mason Jar

Look to chalkboard paint to personalize the Mason jar. Simply create a square, rectangular, or circular area in the center of your jar with the use of tape to secure your boundaries. Paint the inside of the created rectangle or circle with the chalkboard paint, and allow it to dry before peeling off the tape. Include some chalk with the gift (secured with twine, perhaps?), and write the recipe name or your friend's name in the chalkboard on the glass.

3. Create Designer Labels

To create a designer label, simply type up the recipe and extra ingredients your gift-receiver requires to create your gift. Next, print out the recipe and choose a swatch of either pretty cloth or pretty wrapping paper. Cut a fine rectangular or square portion from the wrapping paper or cloth, and then hot glue gun the printed recipe to the cloth or the wrapping paper. Cut a hole in the corner of the cloth with a hole puncher, and position the designer label around the jar with the use of twine or ribbon.

4. Look to Ribbon

Different colored ribbons can be used to attach the designer labels, secure the cloth to the top of the jar, or simply to create designs further down the jar. The ribbon lasts forever and can be curled with a quick twist of your scissors for a flirty effect.

5. Attach a Small Spoon to the Side of a Pre-Made Dessert with Pretty Ribbon.

If you've made a dessert already that's ready to eat in the jar, simply tie a pretty wooden spoon to the side of your jar utilizing some ribbon or twine. The spoon is a beautiful extra element in the overall design of your gift.

6. Look to Printable Jar Labels

The Internet provides a plethora of options to decorate your jar labels, as well. You can choose your colors and your patterns, and you can write your recipe in the blank area. Print out the label and attach the label to your jar with ribbon or twine.

Tips to Fill Your Gift Jars

To fill up your jar appropriately, you should try to utilize a funnel (or a homemade funnel made from a paper tube). Pour the ingredients through the funnel to allow the layers to settle nearly at the bottom. After you layer each ingredient, tamp down each layer with the bottom of a clean screwdriver or a meat tenderizer.

Look to the following 30 recipes to maximize your gift-giving experience!

CHAPTER #2
decadent cookies
——— and bars

Decadent Chocolate Chip Cookies in a Jar

Ingredients:

1 ½ cups all-purpose flour

1 tsp. salt

1 tsp. baking soda

1 cup brown sugar

½ cup white sugar

1 ½ cups semi-sweet chocolate chips

Directions:

Begin by bringing together the baking soda, the salt, and the flour in a large bowl. Stir these ingredients together.

In the bottom of a 1-quart jar, pour this flour mixture. On top of the flour mixture, layer the chocolate chips, the white sugar, and the brown sugar. This order is very attractive in the jar, but feel free to experiment with other orders.

Attach the following recipe to the jar:

Extra Ingredients:

1 ½ sticks butter

1 egg

1 tsp. vanilla

Begin by preheating the oven to 375 degrees Fahrenheit. Beat together the one and a half sticks of butter, the egg, and the vanilla in a large bowl.

Next, toss in the cookie jar mixture and stir well. Drop the created mixture into small balls on a baking sheet, and bake each batch for about ten minutes. The cookies should be golden brown. Allow the cookies to cool, and enjoy!

Cranberry and White Chocolate Oatmeal Cookies in a Jar

Ingredients:
¼ cup white sugar
½ cup brown sugar
¾ cup all-purpose flour
¼ tsp. baking soda
¼ tsp. baking powder
¼ tsp. salt
1 ¼ cup oatmeal
1 ¼ cup white chocolate chips
¾ cup dried cranberries

Directions:
Begin by pouring the white sugar at the bottom of the jar. Make sure that the white sugar is flat at the bottom.

Next, add the brown sugar layer, and even that out, as well.

To the side, mix together baking soda, flour, baking powder, and salt. Stir well, and add this mixture to the jar. Tamp this down, as well. In various layers, add the white chocolate chips, the oats, and the cranberries. Make sure that each layer is flat across for greater aesthetic.

Attach the following recipe to the jar:
Extra Ingredients:
½ cup butter
1 egg
1 tsp. vanilla

Begin by preheating the oven to 375 degrees Fahrenheit.

Next, beat together the butter, the vanilla, and the egg in a large bowl. Add the created cookie mix, and stir until you've created a full, creamy cookie batter. Cover this mixture and allow it to refrigerate for about twenty minutes.

Drop each small tablespoon-sized ball of cookie dough on a baking sheet and bake the cookies for about ten minutes. Enjoy.

Gluten-Free Dutch Chocolate Brownies in a Jar

Ingredients:

1 1/8 cup gluten-free all-purpose flour (I used Bob's Red Mill)

1 tsp. salt

3 tbsp. brown sugar

½ cup white sugar

3 tbsp. Dutch cocoa powder

½ tsp. espresso powder

5 ounces dark chocolate chips

Directions:

Begin by bringing together the flour and salt, and stirring them well. Pour this flour mixture into the bottom of a 3 ½ cup sized jar. Layer the ingredients as such: brown sugar, white sugar, Dutch cocoa powder, espresso powder, and dark chocolate chips.

Attach the following recipe to the jar:

Extra Ingredients:

½ cup vanilla yogurt

2 eggs

Begin by melting the top-layer chocolate chips in a microwavable bowl. Allow the chocolate to cool, and then add the yogurt.

Whisk together this mixture with the two eggs. Add the remaining dry ingredients slowly, stirring as you go along.

Transfer this brownie mixture into a baking tin and bake the brownies for thirty minutes. Allow the brownies to cool, and enjoy.

Extra Gooey Monster M&M Brownies in a Jar

Ingredients:

1 ½ cups white sugar

1 ¼ cups all-purpose flour

1 cup baking cocoa

¼ tsp. salt

½ cup optional walnuts

1 cup M&Ms

Directions:

Layer out the above ingredients in your one-quart jar. Mix together the flour and the salt, and place the flour on the bottom. Next, add the baking cocoa, white sugar, walnuts, and the M&Ms.

Attach the following recipe to the jar:

Extra ingredients:

¾ cup butter

2 eggs

3 tbsp. water

2 ½ tbsp. vanilla

Begin by preheating your oven to 350 degrees Fahrenheit.

Next, pour the dry mixture into a big mixing bowl, and add the butter, eggs, water, and the vanilla. Stir the ingredients together to create a batter. Bake the brownies for twenty-five minutes, and cool. Enjoy!

Super-Simple Summertime Lemon Cookies in a Jar

Ingredients:

1 box of lemon supreme cake mix

12 ounces white chocolate chips

Directions:

Simply pour the lemon cake mix at the bottom of your 1-quart jar and layer the chocolate chips overtop.

Next, decorate your jar and add the following recipe:

Extra Ingredients:

2 eggs

½ cup vegetable oil

Begin by preheating your oven to 350 degrees Fahrenheit.

Next, bring together the oil and the eggs and stir well. Add the jar's contents and continue to stir until you've mixed the dough thoroughly.

Drop each of the cookies onto a baking sheet and cook them for nine minutes. Enjoy!

Buttery Butterscotch Cookies in a Jar

Ingredients:

1 cup butterscotch chips
1 ¼ cups all-purpose flour
1/3 cup rice cereal
1 tsp. baking soda
½ tsp. baking powder
½ cup oatmeal
1/3 cup white sugar

Directions:

Begin by layering the above ingredients in the following order, making sure that each layer is straight across in the jar:

1. Half of the butterscotch chips
2. Rice cereal
3. All-purpose flour
4. Baking soda
5. Baking powder
6. Brown sugar
7. Remainder of the butterscotch chips
8. Oatmeal
9. White sugar

Next, place the following recipe on the jar:

Extra ingredients:
½ cup butter

1 egg
3 tbsp. water

Begin by preheating the oven to 350 degrees Fahrenheit.

Next, bring together the butter, egg, and the water in a large bowl. Add the whole jar's mix to the wet mixture and stir well.

Create small, round cookie dough balls on a baking sheet, and bake the cookies for twelve minutes. Enjoy.

Chocolate Chip Blondie Mix in a Jar

Ingredients:

1 ¼ cup all-purpose flour

½ tsp. salt

½ cup semisweet chocolate chips

1 cup brown sugar

½ cup peanut butter chips

Directions:

Begin by mixing together the flour and the salt and pouring this mixture into the bottom of the jar. Make sure to align the bottom to make it flat across. Top the flour with the chocolate chips, then place a layer of the peanut butter chips over the chocolate. Next, wrap up the brown sugar in a plastic bag or in some parchment paper and drop the brown sugar overtop the chips.

Decorate the jar however you please, and attach the following recipe instructions:

Extra Ingredients:

1 stick of butter

1 tsp. vanilla

1 egg

½ tsp. salt

Begin by preheating the oven to 350 degrees Fahrenheit.

Next, pour the chocolate chips and the peanut butter chips into one bowl and the flour mixture into a separate bowl. Keep the wrapped brown sugar to the side. Melt the butter and combine the butter with the brown sugar. Add the egg and continue to stir. Lastly, add the vanilla.

Pour the dry flour mixture to the butter mixture and stir until just combined. Toss in the chocolate and peanut butter goodies, and pour the batter into a baking pan. Allow the blondies to bake for twenty-five minutes, enjoy.

CHAPTER #3

scrumptious cakes
in a jar

Autumn Carrot Cake Mix in a Jar

Ingredients:

2 ½ cups white sugar

2 ½ cups all-purpose flour

½ cup chopped walnuts

1 tbsp. cinnamon

2 tsp. baking soda

½ tsp. nutmeg

Directions:

Create the above carrot cake recipe in a jar by formulating a flour and baking soda layer on the bottom of a one-quart jar; create a nutmeg flavor after that; follow the nutmeg layer with white sugar; follow this with cinnamon and walnuts.

Attach the following recipe to the jar:

Extra Ingredients:

1 1/3 cups vegetable oil

2 ½ tsp. vanilla

3 eggs

8 ounces crushed pineapple

3 ¼ cups sliced and grated carrots

Preheat your oven to 350 degrees Fahrenheit.

Pour the carrot cake mix into a large bowl, and add the eggs, oil, pineapple, and carrots. Stir this mixture together until it's completely mixed.

Pour this prepared mixture into a cake pan and bake the cake for fifty minutes. Allow the cake to cook until a toothpick that is inserted in the middle comes out clean. Dust the cake with confectioners' sugar.

Luscious Lemon Cake in a Jar

Ingredients:

2 ¼ cups all-purpose flour

½ tsp. baking soda

¾ tsp. baking powder

1 tsp. salt

1 ½ cups white sugar

2 tbsp. grated lemon zest

1 cup dried cranberries

Directions:

Begin by bringing together flour, baking soda, baking powder, and the salt in a small bowl. Stir well. Next, pour this mixture into the bottom of the one-quart Mason jar. Place the cranberries overtop of the flour mixture followed by the lemon zest. Top the lemon zest with the white sugar, and cap the jar.

Next, add the following recipe to the jar:

Extra ingredients:

½ cup butter

3 eggs

3 tbsp. lemon juice

1 cup buttermilk

Extra powdered sugar, for sprinkling.

Begin by preheating the oven to 350 degrees Fahrenheit.

Next, bring together all the wet ingredients: butter, eggs, lemon juice, and the buttermilk, in a large bowl. Stir well. Pour the dry jar mix into the wet ingredients and continue to stir until you formulate your cake mix.

Pour the batter into a cake pan and bake the cake for thirty-five minutes. When you insert a toothpick into the center, it should come up clean. Enjoy with a sprinkle of powdered sugar.

Devil's Best Food Cake in a Jar

Ingredients:
2 ¼ cups all-purpose flour
½ tsp. baking powder
1 ½ tsp. baking soda
2 ¼ cups white sugar
1 cup cocoa powder
1 bag semi-sweet chocolate chips

Directions:
Begin by bringing together the flour, baking powder, and baking soda. Stir well, and pour this mixture into the bottom of the one-quart Mason jar.

Next, follow this layer with the cocoa powder, white sugar, and the semi-sweet chocolate chips.

Close the jar and position the following recipe on it, as well:
Extra ingredients:
10 tbsp. butter
2 tsp. vanilla
3 eggs
1 ½ cups water
¼ cup milk

Preheat the oven to 350 degrees Fahrenheit.

Begin by bringing together the wet ingredients in a large mixing bowl: butter, vanilla, eggs, water, and milk. Stir well, and then add the jar cake mix. Continue to stir until you create your batter.

Pour the batter into a cake pan and bake the cake for about forty minutes. The cake should begin to pull off from the surrounding pan. Enjoy this delicious cake with the frosting of your choice!

Ready-to-Eat Red Velvet Cake in a Jar

Ingredients:

1 cup cake flour

1 tsp. salt

2 ½ tbsp. cocoa powder

2/3 cup vegetable oil

1 egg

1 cup sugar

2 tbsp. red food dye

1 tsp. vanilla

½ tsp. baking soda

½ cup buttermilk

1 tsp. vinegar

Cream Cheese Frosting Ingredients:

8 ounces of cream cheese

3 ½ cups confectioners' sugar

3 ½ tbsp. butter

2 tsp. vanilla

Directions:

Begin by preheating the oven to 350 degrees Fahrenheit. Place paper liners in cupcake tins. Next, stir together the salt, cocoa powder, and the cake flour.

To the side, mix together the oil and the sugar. Add the egg and stir until the ingredients are completely assimilated.

Next, add the vanilla and continue to stir as you add the red food dye. Pour the flour mixture and the buttermilk into the bowl and continue to stir. Do not over mix the ingredients.

To the side, bring together the baking soda and the vinegar in a small bowl. Stir prior to adding the mixture to the greater mixture. Continue to stir. Afterwards, divide the batter into the twelve muffin tins and bake the muffins for twenty-four minutes. If you insert a toothpick into the muffin, it should come out completely clear.

Next, focus on your cream cheese frosting while the muffins are cooling.
Stir together with either your big spoon or your mixer the cream cheese and the butter. Slowly add the confectioners' sugar and the vanilla and mix until you've created your perfect frosting.

Next, assemble the jars.

Slice each of the created cupcakes in horizontal pieces—like you're creating two layers. Each cupcake should yield about three layers.

Drop a layer of cupcake into the bottom of one of your jars. Place a layer of cream cheese frosting over the cupcake layer and then drop another layer of red velvet over the frosting. Continue to layer until you hit the top of your jar. Top the jar and decorate the jar as you please for all gift-giving festivities.

Gluten-Free Fall Time Pumpkin Pancake Mix in a Jar

Ingredients:

2 cups gluten-free rolled oats, ground up in the food processor

1 lemon's zest

1 tsp. baking soda

½ tsp. salt

1 tsp. ginger

1 ½ tsp. cinnamon

½ tsp. cloves

1 tsp. nutmeg

3 tbsp. brown sugar

Directions:

Bring all the above ingredients together and stir well. Pour them into a one-quart jar, and decorate the jar as you please.

Add the following instructions to the jar:

Extra ingredients:

1 cup pure pumpkin puree

2 tbsp. melted butter

2 eggs

½ cup milk

1 cup of pancake mix from the already prepared jar

Begin by whisking together the milk, butter, and the pumpkin puree. Add 2 eggs and continue to stir.

Next, add one cup of the jar mixture into the butter mixture, and mix the two forces together until they're just combined. Don't over mix. Allow the mixture to sit out for fifteen minutes.

Next, heat up a skillet and grease up the pan.

Add a forth of a cup of batter to the skillet and cook the first side of the pancake for three minutes. Flip the pancake and cook the other side for one and a half minutes. Each side should be golden brown. Enjoy immediately!

CHAPTER #4

breads, muffins and scones

in a jar

Zesty Orange and Cranberry Oatmeal Scone in a Jar

Ingredients:

1 cup white flour

¼ cup whole wheat flour

¼ tsp. salt

2 tsp. baking powder

1 ¼ cups oats

2 tsp. orange peel zest

1/3 cup brown sugar

¼ cup skim milk powder

¾ cup dried cranberries

Directions:

Begin by layering the ingredients in a one-quart jar. Before doing this, you'll need to mix together the white flour, salt, and the baking powder. You'll also need to mix together the orange zest and the brown sugar.

The proper order of the scone mix is the following:

1. White flour with salt and baking powder
2. Whole wheat flour
3. Skim milk powder
4. Oats
5. Brown sugar with orange zest

6. Cranberries

Next, attach the following recipe to your jar:
Extra ingredients:
1/3 cup butter
1/3 cup water
1 egg

First, preheat the oven to 400 degrees Fahrenheit.

Next, empty out the one-quart jar with the recipe inside, and set the cranberries to the side.

Cut the third cup of butter into the dry mixture. Next, add the egg, the water, and the cranberries. You should mix the ingredients until you create a soft dough.

Place this dough onto a flat surface, and divide the dough in half. Formulate each piece of dough into a round ball. Next, pat the balls into circles with about five inches of diameter on the baking sheet.

Place the circles an inch apart on the baking sheet. Cut the circles into six wedges each, and brush the top of the scone mixture with sugar.

Bake the scones for fifteen minutes until they are browned. Enjoy warm!

Mushy Marshmallow Mega Muffins

Ingredients:

1 4/5 cups all-purpose flour

2 ½ tsp. baking powder

¾ cup cocoa powder

½ cup white sugar

1/3 cup chocolate chips

1/3 cup mini marshmallows

Directions:

Begin by layering the ingredients above in the following order:

1. Baking powder
2. Flour
3. Cocoa powder
4. White sugar
5. Chocolate chips
6. Mini marshmallows

Next, attach the following recipe to the jar:

Extra ingredients:

1 1/3 cup milk

6 tbsp. melted butter

1 egg

Begin by preheating the oven to 375 degrees Fahrenheit.

Next, combine together the milk, egg, and butter. Bring the jar ingredients into a large bowl along with the wet ingredients.

Spoon the mixture into the muffin tins, and bake the muffins for twenty-five minutes. Allow the muffins to cool for fifteen minutes prior to diving in! Enjoy.

Holiday Party Cranberry Bread in a Jar

Ingredients:

1 ¼ cup whole wheat flour

1 tsp. baking soda

½ tsp. baking powder

¼ cup brown sugar

1/3 cup raisins or dried cranberries

1 tsp. cinnamon

½ cup oatmeal

¼ cup diced walnuts

Directions:

Begin by placing the whole wheat flour at the bottom of the one-quart jar. Administer the baking soda and the powder to the top of the flour. Add the brown sugar followed by the dried cranberries. Top the cranberries with the walnuts, the cinnamon, and then the oatmeal. Close the jar, and decorate it how you please.

Next, attach the following recipe to refine the final product:

Extra Ingredients:

½ cup buttermilk

1 egg

¼ cup water

2 tbsp. maple syrup

2 tbsp. butter

Begin by dumping out the jar mix into a large mixing bowl. Next, pour in the water and the buttermilk, and cover up the bowl. Place the bowl in a corner of your kitchen and allow it to sit for twenty-four hours.

The next day, preheat your oven to 350 degrees Fahrenheit. To the bowl, add the maple syrup, egg, and the melted butter. Use a whisk to bring all the ingredients together.

Pour the batter into a bread pan and allow it to bake for thirty minutes. Serve warm, and enjoy!

Pumpkin Raisin Bread in a Jar

Ingredients:

1 1/3 cups all-purpose flour

1 tsp. baking soda

3 tsp. pumpkin pie spice

1 tsp. salt

1 1/3 cups sugar

½ cup raisins

Directions:

Begin by stirring together the flour, baking soda, and the salt together in a large bowl. Pour the mixture into the very bottom of a one-quart jar, and flatten out the top.

Next, place a layer of pumpkin pie spice followed by the cups of sugar.

Top the jar with the raisins, and attach the following recipe instructions:

Extra Ingredients:

15 ounces pure pumpkin

½ cup vegetable oil

¼ cup orange juice

2 eggs

Begin by preheating your oven to 350 degrees Fahrenheit.

Next, stir together the pure pumpkin, oil, orange juice, and the eggs. Add the jar contents to the bowl and stir until the wet mixture moistens the dry mixture. Make sure not to over-mix.

Next, pour the mixture into the bottom of a 9x5 bread pan and bake the bread in the preheated oven for sixty-five minutes. Remember to allow the bread to cool for ten minutes prior to serving.

Bursting Banana Bread Mix in a Jar

Ingredients:

¾ cup white flour

1 tsp. baking soda

1 ½ tbsp. dry buttermilk powder

1 tsp. cinnamon

½ tsp. salt

1/3 cup brown sugar

½ cup oat bran

1/3 cup whole wheat pastry flour

1 cup diced walnuts

Directions:

Pour the above ingredients in the following order:

1. Stirred together white flour, baking soda, and buttermilk powder.
2. Brown sugar
3. Whole wheat pastry flour
4. Oat bran
5. Rolled Oats
6. Walnuts

Next, attach the following recipe instructions to the jar:

Extra Ingredients:

2 eggs

1/3 cup water

½ cup applesauce

2 tbsp. vegetable oil

1 tsp. vanilla

4 mashed bananas

Begin by preheating the oven to 350 degrees Fahrenheit.

Next, mix together eggs, water, applesauce, vegetable oil, vanilla, and the mashed bananas. Add the wet ingredients to the jar's already-mixed dry ingredients. Stir well, and spread the batter into a loaf pan.

Bake the bread for sixty minutes and allow the bread to cool for fifteen minutes prior to serving. Enjoy.

Cinnamon Spice Christmas Muffin Mix in a Jar

Ingredients:

2 ¼ cups flour

2 tsp. baking powder

1 tsp. baking soda

1 cup sugar

2 tsp. cinnamon

½ tsp. nutmeg

½ tsp. ginger

¼ tsp. cloves

Dash of salt

Directions:

Begin by mixing together flour, baking powder, salt, and baking soda. Pour this mixture into the bottom of a one-quart jar.

Next, add a layer of cinnamon, a layer of white sugar, a layer of nutmeg, a layer of cloves, and a layer of ginger.

Attach the following recipe outline to the decorated jar:

Extra Ingredients:

½ cup vegetable oil

2 eggs

½ cup water

1 ½ sticks of butter

Begin by preheating the oven to 350 degrees Fahrenheit.

Mix together the wet ingredients in a large mixing bowl. Then, add the dry ingredients from the jar into the wet mixture, and stir them together. Pour the batter into twelve muffin tins, and bake the muffins for eighteen minutes. When you insert your toothpick into the center, you should remove a clean toothpick.

Allow the muffins to cool. Enjoy!

CHAPTER #5

delicious drinks
in a jar

Christmas Eve Cocoa

Ingredients:

1 cup cocoa powder

¾ cup powdered milk

1 tsp. salt

¾ cup white sugar

½ cup peppermint candy

1/3 cup chocolate chips

Directions:

Begin by crushing up the peppermint candies.

Next, create the layers in a one-quart jar by assimilating the following order:

1. Powdered milk
2. Cocoa powder
3. Sugar
4. Salt
5. Peppermint candy
6. Chocolate chips

Attach the following instructions to the jar:

Mix together the jar ingredients in a large bowl. One serving requires a third cup of cocoa mix with one cup of boiling water. Store the rest of the mixture for a later cocoa date!

Spiced Cider and Tea in a Jar

Ingredients:

2 cups orange drink mix (like Tang)

2/3 cup instant iced tea mix

1 package lemonade mix

2 tsp. cinnamon

2 ¼ cups sugar

1 ½ tsp. cloves

Directions:

Begin by mixing all the ingredients together in a bowl. Pour the ingredients into a one-quart jar and package up the jar to make it beautiful for gift-giving.

Next, write-out the following instructions for your gift recipient:

Add one tablespoon of this cider mix to one cup of hot water. Alternately, add one tablespoon of the mix with one cup of hot apple cider to make hot cider. Enjoy.

Chai Tea Latte Mix in a Jar

Ingredients:

1 cup sugar

1 cup dry milk powder

1 cup powdered coffee creamer

2 ¼ cups instant tea

2 tsp. cinnamon

2 ½ tsp. ginger

1 tsp. clove

1 ¼ tsp. nutmeg

1 ¼ tsp. allspice

1 tsp. cardamom

Directions:

Begin by mixing together the creamer, milk powder, sugar, instant tea, cinnamon, ginger, cloves, cardamom, allspice, and the nutmeg.

Blend the ingredients together in a food processor, and place the mixture in a one-quart jar.

Attach the following recipe to the jar:

Bring three tablespoons of the Chai Tea Latte mixture into one cup of hot water and stir well. Relax and enjoy.

Italian Cappuccino in a Jar

Ingredients:
1 cup instant coffee mix
½ cup white sugar
1 cup powdered creamer
1 tsp. cinnamon
1 ¼ cup powdered chocolate drink
½ tsp. nutmeg

Directions:
Begin by processing the instant coffee in a food processor.

To the side, mix together the chocolate mix, creamer, sugar, processed coffee, nutmeg, and the cinnamon. Mix the ingredients together and add them to two 12-ounce sized jars.

Attach the following recipe instructions to the jar:
Mix together three tablespoons of powder with six ounces of boiling water.

DIY Mulled Wine in a Jar

Ingredients:

6 whole star anise

3 tbsp. whole allspice berries

7 3-inch cinnamon sticks

2 tbsp. complete cloves

1 ½ tbsp. green cardamom pods

1 ¼ tsp. black peppercorns

1 bottle of red wine

1 orange

Directions:

Begin by bringing together the cinnamon sticks and the star anise in a plastic bag and rolling over them with a rolling pin to completely crush them together. Add this crushed mixture to the rest of the spices, and place this mixture in a one-ounce jar.

Decorate the jar as you please and give the gift with an orange, a bottle of wine, and the following instructions:

In order to mull the wine, you will need:

1 tbsp. of the spice mix from this jar

1 cheesecloth square

2 tbsp. maple syrup or honey

1 orange's worth of zest and juice

1 bottle of red wine

Begin by placing one tablespoon of the mixture in the very middle of a square cheesecloth and bring the cheesecloth together in the middle, tying it with the string.

Place the cheesecloth spice bag in a saucepan with honey, orange juice, orange zest, and the bottle of red wine.

Allow the mixture to steam, making sure not to allow it to boil. Continue to stir until the honey's sugar has completely dissolved. Enjoy.

CHAPTER #6
sweet snacks
in a jar

Crunch and Munch Christmas Granola

Ingredients:

2 ½ cups oatmeal
1/3 cup pumpkin seeds
1/3 cup sunflower seeds
3 tbsp. maple syrup
2 tbsp. sesame seeds
2 tbsp. honey
4 tbsp. maple syrup
2 ½ tsp. vanilla
3 tbsp. coconut oil (melted)
4 tbsp. peanut butter
2 tsp. cinnamon
½ cup dried cranberries

Directions:

Preheat the oven to 350 degrees Fahrenheit.
Begin by stirring together all the oats, pumpkin seeds, sunflower seeds, and sesame seeds.

In a different bowl, stir together the honey, maple syrup, melted coconut oil, peanut butter, cinnamon, and vanilla. Mix the ingredients well, and pour this liquid over the oats. Stir well in order to completely coat the oats.

Next, spread the oats over a baking pan and bake for twenty-five minutes. Every ten minutes, stir the granola around the pan a little bit.

Allow the granola to completely cool, and then add the cranberries. Place the granola in a 12-ounce jar and decorate as you please.

Slow Cooker Grandma-Brand Apple Butter

Ingredients:

10 apples, both sweet and tart

1 ¼ cups maple syrup

2 ½ cups apple juice

1 tsp. cinnamon

1/3 cup lemon juice

½ tsp. nutmeg

¼ tsp. ginger

½ tsp. salt

¼ tsp. allspice

Directions:

Begin by coring and peeling all the apples and slicing and dicing them. Place them in the slow cooker along with the other ingredients. Stir the apples well, and then cover the slow cooker and cook the apples on HIGH for one hour.

Afterwards, reduce the heat to a low setting and cook the apples for one more hour.

Stir the apples and place the lid on the slow cooker to allow steam to escape—putting it a little bit crooked on the top. Continue to cook the apples for another nine hours on low, allowing this steam to spurt out.

Afterwards, turn off the slow cooker and stir the butter. You can food process this apple butter to formulate a smoother texture, but you don't necessarily have to if you like chunkier varieties.

Afterwards, place the apple butter in 12 half-pint mason jars and pretty one or two of them up to give to friends and relatives. You can store the apple butter in the fridge for two weeks or in the freezer for up to one year.

No-Grain Healthful Nutty Fruit Bars in a Jar

Ingredients:
½ cup unsweetened coconut flakes
1 cup diced almonds
½ cup dried cranberries

Directions:
Begin by chopping up almonds, fruit, and the coconut flakes. Position them in the following layer: first the almonds, then the cranberries, then the coconut flakes.

Next, create the following instructions and place them with the jar:
Extra Ingredients:
1/3 cup honey
3 tsp. almond butter

Begin by preheating the oven to 300 degrees Fahrenheit.

Next, mix together the almond butter and the honey. Allow this mixture to be completely smooth.

Afterwards, add the jar ingredients to the bowl and stir well.

Place this mixture into a baking dish and bake the bars for twenty minutes. Allow the bars to cool for one hour, and then cool them in the freezer for thirty minutes. Cut up the fruit bars with a sharp knife, and enjoy!

Gingerbread Snap Caramel Corn in a Jar

Ingredients:

7 cups popped popcorn
¼ tsp. salt
1 cup brown sugar
½ cup butter
¼ cup molasses
1/8 cup corn syrup
1/2 tbsp. ginger
½ tsp. baking soda
1 tsp. cinnamon

Directions:

Begin by preheating the oven to 250 degrees Fahrenheit.

Next, place all of the popped popcorn into a 13x9 inch pan. To the side, mix together the butter, salt, brown sugar, molasses, corn syrup, cinnamon, and ginger in a big saucepan. Allow it to heat up on medium until the full mixture starts to boil. Allow it to boil for five minutes. Next, remove the saucepan from the stove and add the baking soda. The baking soda will force the mixture to foam.

Pour this frothy spiced mix onto the popcorn in the prepared pan and mix the popcorn to coat it with the stuff. Bake the pan for one hour, making sure to stir the mixture every fifteen minutes. Cool the mixture completely.

Store the mixture in a one-quart jar and give it to family and friends for the holidays! (Keep a little for yourself; trust me, it's outrageously delicious.)

Chewy Cherry Praline Snack in a Jar

Ingredients:

3 ½ cups frosted flakes

4 ½ cups puffy corn cereal

1 cup brown sugar

1/3 cup butter

½ cup corn syrup

¼ tsp. salt

1 tsp. vanilla

¼ tsp. baking soda

1 ¼ cup dried cherries

Directions:

Begin by preheating your oven to 350 degrees Fahrenheit.

Next, mix together the puffy corn cereal and the frosted flakes in a big mixing bowl.

To the side, boil together the brown sugar, butter, corn syrup, and salt. Allow the mixture to boil over medium heat for about six minutes.

Remove the mixture from the heat and add the baking soda and the vanilla. Pour this mixture over the already prepared cereal mixture and stir well.

Place the mixture in a baking dish or pan and bake for fifteen minutes.

After the mixture cools for ten minutes, stir the dried cherries into the mixture and allow it to continue to cool. Store the snack in a one-quart jar to give to family and friends. Enjoy.

Sugar and Spice Pecans in a Jar

Ingredients:

½ tsp. garlic powder

1/8 tsp. cayenne pepper

1/8 tsp. white pepper

1/8 tsp. black pepper

½ tsp. ginger

½ cup butter

2 tbsp. Worcestershire sauce

4 ½ cups sliced pecans

Directions:

Begin by combining together the spices, butter, Worcestershire sauce, and the peppers. Place the sliced pecans in a slow cooker and add the butter mixture over the pecans. Stir the pecans well, and cover the slow cooker.

Cook the pecans on low heat for two hours. After two hours, stir them well, and cover the slow cooker once more. Cook on HIGH for thirty minutes, and remove the pecans from the slow cooker.

Allow the pecans to cool and then store them in jars to gift to friends and family.

Chocolate Apricots Dippers in a Jar

Ingredients:

5 4-ounce bars of chopped baking chocolate
2 tbsp. butter
2 ½ tbsp. canola oil
2 ½ tbsp. heavy cream
1 pound dried apricots

Directions:

Begin by lining your baking sheets with parchment paper.

Place the oil, chocolate, butter, and the heavy cream together in a saucepan. Melt the ingredients slowly, stirring occasionally, over medium heat. The chocolate mixture should be completely smooth when you take it off the stovetop.

Next, dip each of the apricots halfway into the chocolate. Place the apricots onto the parchment papers, and then refrigerate the dried fruits for about one hour.

After the chocolate has dried to the apricots, place the apricots in your gift jars, and decorate the jars as you please.

Conclusion

DIY Gifts in Jars comes to your gift-giving rescue. Never before has your holiday season or your birthday gift giving seemed so easy, and never before have your friends and family been more pleased. Cookies, brownies, blondies, cakes, breads, scones—even crunchy snacks!—come together in beautiful mason jars. Each Mason jar can be elaborately decorated to suit your or your friend's personality, and each recipe can be suited for the season. Opt for red velvet cake on Valentine's Day, for example; or create apple butter for your friend's Thanksgiving Dinner party. Not a single store exists in the world that can better suit your holiday and birthday gift-giving needs. Head home, and start your DIY creations. Bring warmth and pleasure to kitchens all over the world, and leave your family looking forward to your jarred presents!